GLO ROSE PRESENTS:

WRAPPING PAPER

Our wrapping paper
matters too.

The birthday of a loved one comes, and we mark it off the calendar. As you go to their favorite store, smiling ear to ear, you pick that special gift. You carefully cut the wrapping paper at home. You use the best tape and delicately bring the pieces together for the neatest presentation. Topping it with a bow for love, you head to your car.

You drive to their house, excited to see their face when they get their gift. At their door and practically bouncing on the balls of your feet, you ring their doorbell and wait for them to answer. The door opens.

They see the beautifully wrapped present outstretched in front of you. Their loved one is standing at the door with a big smile and a present...looking like they just fell out of bed.

Yes, I went there!!!

So the question is: Why do we put more care into the wrapping paper on a gift than the wrapping paper we put on ourselves? We hold a gift in ourselves, yet we take little thought into how we present it to the world.

Let's face it, you rarely see a celebrity or famous person dressed for the red carpet, or even a sports game, in clothes that would get them a one-way ticket to the worst-dressed list. Yes, you'll say, "But they have money and a stylist." True, but we have Target, Walmart, and the internet.😉 We even have Stitch Fix if, like me, you have no fashion sense.

So, let's get into it. The gifts of our talents should always be wrapped to impress. I'm not saying you have to dress to the nines. However, a little extra thought about what we want to present to the world before we leave the house couldn't hurt either.

Consider this: you shop for some jeans in PJ pants, a messy ponytail, and a T-shirt with slippers. You see someone you really like. What do you think they think of your outfit? Or what if you are an over-achieving straight 'A' student who comes to school in too tight and revealing clothing? Are people seeing your brains or your bum? True, what we wear shouldn't matter, but unfortunately, it does.

So, make sure to let what you show the world be a message to remember. Let the words 'classy,' 'respectable,' and 'impressive' be what they see before they know your name.

CONTENTS

Shoes

Shoes: It's All

About the Base

Chapter 1: Shoes

Just like with any gift, you want to start with the base. So let's talk about shoes. Get comfortable because I love a good movie reference. Let's start this chapter with a classic.

"Mama always said there's an awful lot you could tell about a person by their shoes: where they're going, where they've been." - Forrest from Forrest Gump

Forest's Mom had a point; we can tell a lot about a person from what is on their feet. First and foremost, while I'm sure many won't agree, we need to address the elephant in the room. Crocs, slides, and house shoes belong only in a few places:

- Beach/Pools
- Showers at the gym
- Decks

- Backyard parties
- A workplace where you stand a lot and need comfortable, durable shoes

  OR
- At home

They are the roll-out-of-bed, keeping-it-way-too-casual, put-in-no-effort shoes. We want the world to take us seriously when we step out of our front door. This includes our dreams, hopes, ambitions, and contributions. Even a trip to the store in Crocs can affect all that.

Therefore, they don't belong in store aisles, most workplaces, or classrooms. Don't give a school presentation in a pair of house shoes. Expect a pass on the next date if you show up with a pair of slip-on sandals and socks.

Shoes can set the tone for the whole day. No matter where you're going, the way your feet look can set an impression on anyone who meets you. How your shoes make you feel can help you stand taller and keep a pep in your step. Look out, world, as you rock your confidence from your head to your toes.

Don't get me wrong; I love a comfortable pair of easy-to-get-on shoes. However, you can have style, positivity, and easy-to-get-on shoes all at the same time. A good pair of boat shoes with those shorts. A modern pair of flats with that dress. Even a stylish pair of wedges with those jeans.

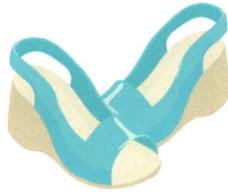

You can enhance or compliment your outfit by selecting the right shoes to fit the situation. Ladies, going window shopping? Rock a nice pair of stylish sandals, modern flats, or fashionable athletic shoes. Gentlemen, going to the store? Wear casual boat shoes, leather-strapped sports sandals, or fashion-forward athletic shoes.

Now, let me let you in on a little something. Gentlemen, a pair of well-maintained leather boots can turn heads. Ladies, a smart pair of low heels or wedges can look striking. Show people you are coming from one place and going somewhere better. Put your best foot forward, pun intended, in the right shoes for your best look.

Lastly, should you ever wear sandals... DON'T DO SO WITH SOCKS!!! I don't know who or why this trend started... BUT STOP IT!

Bottoms

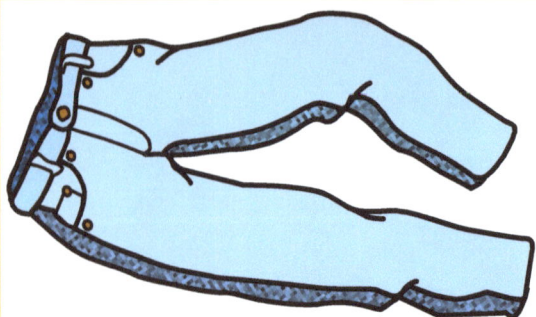

Bottoms: Can maketh or breaketh a person

Chapter 2: Bottoms

Ladies first. I have two questions for you:

- Why are your pants so see-thru that we know the color of your underwear?

OR

- Why are your skirts short enough to leave very little to the imagination?

Gentlemen, you're up next:

- Why do you wear your pants tight enough so everyone knows how you feel at a moment's notice?

OR

- Why do you think we need to see the color and type of your underwear?

Now, everyone:

- Why do you think bed pants should be worn in public?

Taking a few of those questions to heart? Well, I am sure they are all questions you have asked yourself while visiting the aisles of the grocery store or the halls of the mall. Questions you asked even while a different question applied to you.

Movie reference, anyone?

"These sweatpants are all that fits me right now." - Regina from Mean Girls

In the movie Mean Girls the popular clique of girls in the school has upheld their power by bad attitudes wrapped in stylish ensembles. When Regina, their leader, gains weight, the only thing that fits her in her closet is a pair of sweatpants.

The image she built to control the school and the clique is tarnished by a simple pair of pink sweatpants.

Confession: I am a jeans girl. 105°F weather to 5°F, I will wear jeans all day and every day. I specifically like flare jeans. I know a little too 70s, though I have been told the straight leg should be more my cut. However, I have been told that jeans aren't for every occasion and, as much as I hate to admit it, they are right.

Pants, skirts, shorts, skorts, and leggings all work in everyday fashion. However, it is how we wear them that maketh the person. Let's look at the key point of every pair of bottoms.

- Fit — They should fit comfortably. This should be done in a way that gives the space needed for comfort and conforms to the lines of the body.

- Length — I'm taking it back to school. Skirts and shorts to the fingertips. Why? Because not all secrets need to be revealed so easily. Let's keep them wanting more.

Think of it this way: once upon a time, it was scandalous to show an ankle. 😉

- Visual - Up on the hips and not too thin, everyone. Let your hips do the talking and not your undergarments.

Your bottoms and how they fit can make or break an outfit and an impression. Let's look back at **Mean Girls.** The effect on Regina not looking her best that one time. A simple pair of sweatpants to destroy her power. Need I say more?

Tops

Tops:

Can say a lot.

Chapter 3: Tops

The hardest part of what to wear every day is the top. There are so many styles to match one pair of bottoms. So how is one to choose the right top? This time, let's go to a childhood favorite.

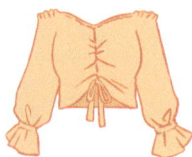

"Now, Ariel, I'm telling ya. If you wanna be a human, the first thing ya gotta do is dress like one. Now, let me see." - Ursula from Little Mermaid

In this scene, Ariel, who has dressed in sea shells and not much else most of her life, is forced to dress like a human for the first time. Having very little idea of what that is, her first attempt is a wrapped-up old sail she finds on the beach. Not the best look to impress a potential interest, let alone a prince.

Her next outfits are much more classy while still being flattering.

Shirts are usually what one sees after the crown (more on that later) and the smile. The shirt speaks volumes, sometimes with enough words on it that you don't have to say a thing. Think of it this way: would you let your parents wear that out of the house? What do I mean? Well, let's take a look.

Think of your parents. Picture them in your mind. Now, think of them in some of the clothes you like to wear. On them, is it too revealing? Is it too tight? Are the words too damaging? Do you think they are sending the wrong message about themselves? Well, this is what they think of you when you walk out of the house in the same clothes. Don't get me wrong. Sometimes, the outfit must be fire because the occasion calls for it. However, it doesn't need to singe your reputation or self-image to be great.

So, a few ground rules. Not too low or too tight. Again, we are leaving something to the imagination. Keeping it moderately comfortable and fitting allows people to see you while admiring your style.

Next, check the wrinkles. While you might have just rolled out of bed with little time to get dressed, it shouldn't look that way. Trust I am the queen of the snooze button. Which is why I prep the night before. I often hang my clothes off my closet door, and nobody knows I got dressed 5 minutes ago.

Lastly, and most importantly, fit the situation. Don't wear a T-shirt under the blazer to a presentation. Don't show too much cleavage in the interview. Even for evening events, you should keep it discreet, smooth, and sharp. Fitting the situation, whether laid-back or buttoned up, can make all the difference in how you are received.

Let's remember Ariel emerges from the ocean in a sparkly blue, above the cleavage, long dress with a modest slit. Not the sea shells.

Hair

Hair: Check Your

Crown

Chapter 4: Hair

Finally, we reached the top, your hair. It's the first thing people see when they see you. I went to an event titled 'Adjusting Your Crown.' I thought of this when I thought about the chapter on hair. It is your crown, the top layer, the tip of your iceberg. It needs to be maintained, and it needs to be all you. Ready for a nerd favorite?

"Your hair has changed. Your appearance now is what we call residual self-image." - Morpheus from The Matrix

Now, what do I mean by the style should be all you? Well, my movie reference will help us dive into your

self-image. Did you ever see *The Matrix*? Well, if not, you should. Anyway, in the movie, Neo is freed into the real world. In the real world, his head is shaved due to all the cords plugged into him. However, when he is reinserted into the Matrix, his mid-length haircut is back. This happened because of how he wanted to see himself.

Now imagine your best self.

- Not the look you are told to have.
- Not the self you pretend to be to fit in.
- Not the "normal" hair color or style.
- Don't even think about what they might think of you at school.

In this image of yourself, answer these questions:

- What color is your hair?
- What length is it?
- Does it have highlights?
- Do you wear hair jewelry?

Develop the images in your mind. Research looks, colors., and styles. Now, see if you can find an app to try the style you find on. Next, please take it to the mirror. Imagine your favorite looks on yourself. Which looks make you smile? Which looks make you glow? Which looks make you wink and say, "Hey, good-looking."

Quick note: Make sure it's a style that will work for a

chill day out or a date night on the town.

Now get to the salon or barber and get that style. Make sure you are satisfied before you leave. Then, with a smile and the new look accomplished, set the next appointment to maintain it.

Your hair is the key to your best smile. When you see yourself in the mirror and get the impulse to wink, you know you look great. So before you leave the house, check the outfit and adjust your crown. Make sure it makes you smile.

Nails

Nails & Hands:

To Clean or Not

to Clean?

Chapter 5: Nails

Now, I know it may seem trivial, but yes, I have dedicated a whole chapter to hands and nails. Not just fingernails but toenails too. Let's keep it real; I appreciate someone who works with their hands. Fixing, building, and creating new ideas from scratch is one of a person's most beautiful talents.

However, your hands shouldn't tell a story you are not ready to share. When you meet a person, you shake their hand in greeting. So, let's start there. Standing with a genuine smile and eye contact, you reach out your right hand, grasp theirs firmly (but not too tight), and give it a kind shake.

Now, here is where the impression comes in. That person you just met looked at your hands before they shook it. They saw any filth on your stained hands and the dirt under your nails. Your hands told a story about you; you don't even know it.

Now, let's talk about toenails. Ladies, imagine this: a handsome boy approaches you at the park while you are with your girlfriends. He has a nice haircut, a modern shirt, a chain around his neck, and fashionable pants. Then you see his toes... which look crusty and dirty in his name-brand sandals - still interested?

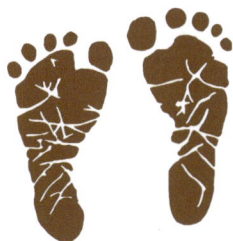

Guys, same question. You see a nice young lady walking around the mall. She has her hair in a sleek updo, wearing a nice dress, thinly applied makeup, and a fashionable necklace with matching earrings. Then you see her feet in an open-toe pair of wedges. The toes look dry, the fingernail polish is chipping, and there is dirt under the nails — Do you still want her number?

Don't misunderstand. I'm not saying you must get a manicure and a pedicure every few weeks. That can be expensive. However, a nail brush and a file are inexpensive and can be kept in a car or purse. 5 minutes in the morning with your coffee, while in the shower, on that break, you take in your car, and you have a set of nails to show off.

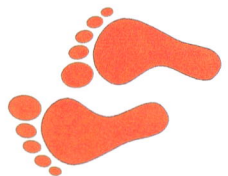

Your mouth, brain, and heart should be what gives the impression about you. However, your visual is often considered before you open your mouth, even down to your nails. So give them some love so they can tell a good story.

Every introduction or encounter is an opportunity. Sometimes you want to take the opportunity, and sometimes you don't. Either way is fine. However, let nothing about you prevent the opportunity from being available. The impression you leave on a person will always be there. So, why not make sure that the impression is a good one? Starting with a handshake from a considerate hand with clean nails.

Words

STAYCALM
workhard
behappy
staystrong
bigdream
enjoylife
focus
behonest
bepositive
moveon
tryagain
achieveit
patient
confidentyourself
positivethinking

Words: The Power to Affect

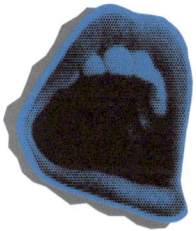

Everything

Chapter 6: Words

Our words have power. Without meaning to, our words can love, heal, encourage, tear down, destroy, and even kill. What you say and how you say it can impact the receiver in ways you can't imagine. That includes saying the wrong thing or writing the wrong response on social media. Look at people who have lost friends, scholarships, and jobs from actions on social media.

Let's skip to the movie reference.

"Do you understand the words that are coming out of my mouth?" - James Carter from Rush Hour

In the movie Rush Hour, Agt Carter makes an assumption about Officer Lee and his ability to speak English. As a result, they get off on the wrong foot and make many mistakes in their investigation. Had this assumption not been made, the movie might have been 60 minutes instead of 98 minutes.

Now, has there ever been a time when that happened to you? Someone assumed, or you assumed, and the wrong words were said? Maybe because of your assumption, you used a harsher or more disrespectful tone than intended.

'Think before you speak' was the line told to me

constantly as a kid. Well, times have changed, so let's expand on that. In today's world, it should be 'Think before you respond.' Yes, thats more like it.

Let's think about social media posts. When we see a post that lights a fire under you, it is hard not to let your fingers dance on the keyboard. When you receive a text full of misrepresented ideals, you have to respond, right? You have to set the record straight, right? WRONG!!!

Sometimes, the question to ask yourself is - 'Does what I'm about to say need to be said?' Will it improve the world or bring more negativity into it? There are times when silence can be louder than any words you can think of. Other times, how you say it can get the point across without burning the bridge.

Today and every day, remember the power of words. Think of words that have been said to you and how they were said. How did that make you feel? Think of words you said to others that might have been misunderstood. How did it feel to have to correct it?

Before you speak or type, give thought to what you are about to say. Words are the hardest thing to take back, so make sure the effect they have is worth it.

Cost

Cost: Hey G, Can We Go Thrift Shopping?

Chapter 7: Cost

As someone who wore hand-me-downs, shared clothes, and wore shoes with holes covered in tape, I get that money can be tight. The price of everything is rising with each passing day. Yet shopping just right can still have you dressed to the nines in affordable gear.

Reference time: One of my favorite songs is Thrift Shop by Macklemore & Ryan Lewis featuring Wanz. The fact that we will spend half the cost of our water bill (or a quarter of our cell phone bill for larger families) can be unbelievable. Thrift shopping can find clothing treasures without the treasure cost. Do you remember that Levis commercial with the thrift store jeans.

People give up great clothes to thrift stores. This is especially true if you shop at thrift shops right after or before the holidays, after spring when people have done their spring cleaning, or at the end of summer when everyone is done having their yard sales.

Then, you will find the nice clothes they can no longer wear, their kids can't fit or don't want, and the clothes might not be in style anymore are all there. For the cost of the clothes and some dry cleaning, you still save money. Even better, no one has to be wise as to where you got the clothes from.

Just because someone dropped a lot of money on

their clothes don't mean you have to.

Before anyone brushes this chapter off, there is another solution to costly clothes. The rich have Gucci, Coach, and Prada. We have Walmart, Target, local shops, and outlet stores. I know notorious deal shoppers who rarely pay full or even half price for anything they buy. Yet, they are some of the most fashionable people I see at work, the mall, or just a friendly get-together.

So, hit the internet and find the image that matches your style the most. Then, hit the store in your price range and find the deals that fit your wallet.

Maintenance

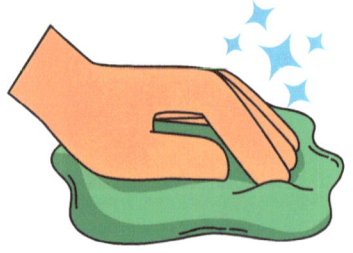

Maintenance:

It might be high maintenance... but it's worth it.

Chapter 8: Maintenance

Now, a fantastic but lost art is the art of clothing maintenance. Let us look to our childhoods for the following movie reference.

"The fabric is comfortable for sensitive skin and can withstand a temperature of 1000° "- Edna Mode
- The Incrediibles

In this scene, Mrs. Incredible is introduced to her family's secret new uniforms. The creator, Edna Mode, gives wearing and care information about each superhero outfit. If you are like me, the tag on clothes is for the size. Everything else is just unnecessary mumbo jumbo.

WRONG

They are actual information to care for your clothes. Even a little clothes and shoe maintenance matter in the impressions made. A little care for clothes today can go a long way to helping them keep their shape and last longer, saving you money in the long run.

Look at it from a different angle, the view of your wallet. As we just got done talking about cost, the longer the last, the less you spend. Don't get it twisted. Buy that great-fitting shirt or stunning shoes if you like them. But the longer they look great, the less tempted you'll be to visit the outlet mall.

Let's first talk about shoes. You might think people who keep shoes in boxes and clean them with toothbrushes are extreme. But their shoes can last for years.

So, a few shoe tips:

- Suede boots - Waterproof them after purchase.
- Leather boots - Use leather oil once a month.
- Athletic shoes - Hand wash and waterproof spray.
- Heels - shoe cream or polish with a soft brush.

Shoes take care of our feet. So, why not take great care of them?

It's clothes turn. Shirts, pants, dresses, and skirts all work together to help show who we are. However, faded, ripped, stained, and stretched in the wrong way can ruin the message as much as any other factor. So, let's talk about essential tips.

So, a few show tips:

- Follow the instructions on the tag.
- Limit dry cleaning.
- Wash inside out.
- Wash in colder water.
- If you can, air dry. If not, dry on a gentler cycle.

  And most important

- Store clothes properly (i.e., hang it up or "store-like" folding for jumpers)

So, to sum it up, keep what helps you feel your best looking its best. Besides, who wants to lose that pair of pants that fits you just right too soon?

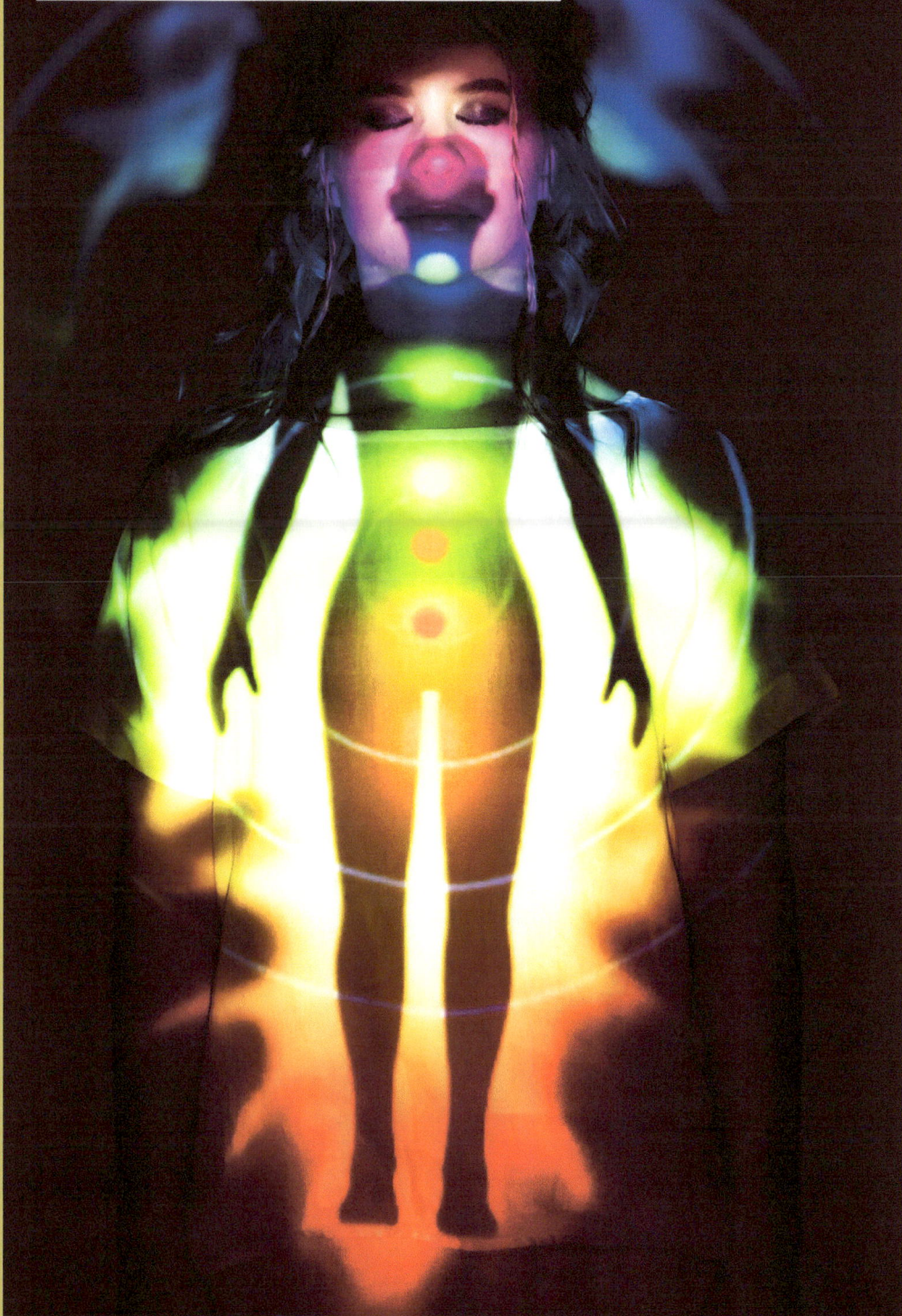

Confidence

Confidence:

Chapter 9: Confidence

Lastly, for the bow on top. I want to talk about confidence. This time, I am going to use a play example. Let's look at Hamilton.

CONFIDENCE

Now, in the play, the narrator and several characters make a habit of calling Alexander Hamilton a bastard and demeaning who he is. Yet even with their doubts and criticisms, especially being told he wasn't on their level, he was always confident about his abilities.

Every word he says and writes exudes his confidence in who he is. It is his hard work sprinkled in confidence that gets him where he wants to be. It gives him the life he wants and a future he never thought possible.

Now, you may ask yourself, do I need the confidence to pick up a tomato from the store? Yes, you do. The way you pick up a tomato can be the gesture that makes someone want to know you better. A future friend or love interest, maybe.

Sidebar: Let us talk about confidence posing and space. Now, hands on the hips, crossed arms, raised eyebrows, facial expressions, and eyes looking all around. All of those can be confidence killers. You may feel good, but the message you are sending is unclear.

So check yourself and how you are taking up space with your expressions. No matter what you do for a living, your level of education, or where you are in life, let that confidence be your bow. So, with your head held up, shoulders back, and swag in your step, keep it up.

Even if it is the day to roll out of bed in your sweats and a wrinkled shirt, and trust me, those days will come, your confidence will still shine from you like a beacon. Rolling in your too-comfortable bedclothes, you rock with the confidence of someone in a sleek tux or fantastic prom dress.

Something to remember: the world will not hesitate to remind you what you look like, where you live, where you work, and most consistently, where you come from. It is up to you to ensure their stamp doesn't determine your path or your future.

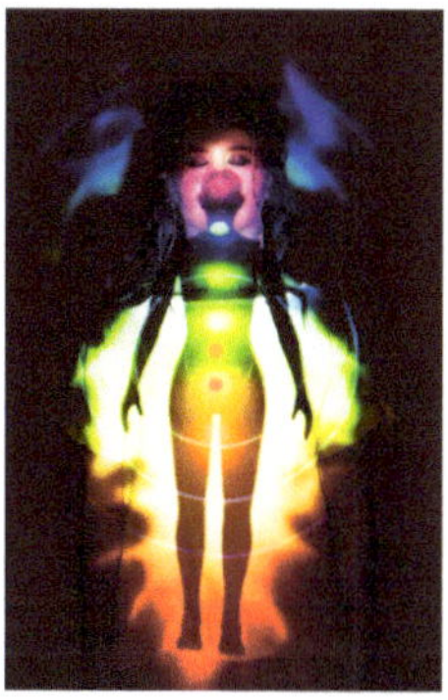

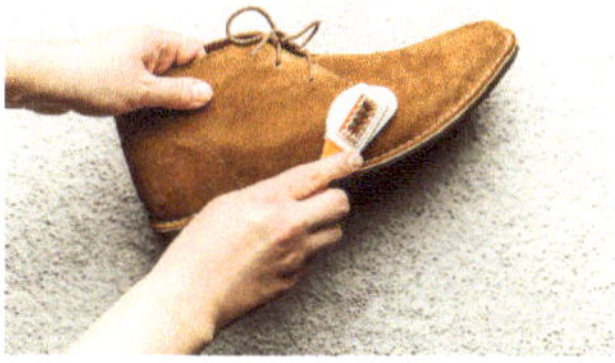

bigdream
behappy
staystrong
enjoylife
workhard
confidentyourself
behappy
patient
focus
STAYCALM
bepositive
STAYCALM
workhard
behonest
tryagain
moveon
staystrong
bepositive
achieveit
drea
confidentyourself
positivethinking
focus

Wrapping Paper

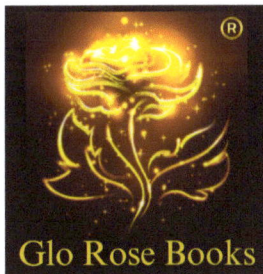

Glo Rose Books

Make sure you check out all this series journals from author
Glo Rose

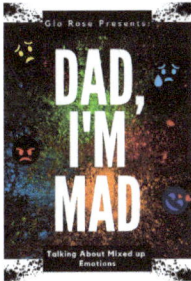

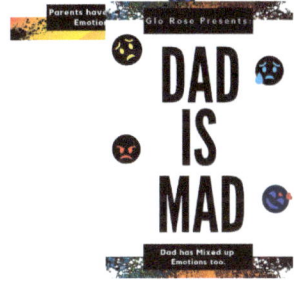

All are available at www. GloRoseBooks.com

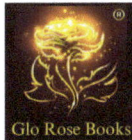

www.ingramcontent.com/pod-product-compliance
Lightning Source LLC
Chambersburg PA
CBHW040513290326

41930CB00036B/116